—PRAISE FOR–

ARMCHAIR LOCOMOTION

"Jen May inhabits space and time differently from you and me: Her El trains *"run on like sentences."* She captures the absence of sound and makes a place for it. Living inside these poems, we discover that it is possible to fall up, wear trees, and love with abandon."
—Bonnie T. Amesquita

"*Armchair Locomotion* is witty and intriguing. Jen May links moments in evocative ways—comparing love to origami, text to cornrows, time to an apple, and contemplating beauty found in life's glimpses."
—Michelle Donfrio

"May takes human condition and stares steely-eyed at it until it bursts into beautiful blossom. You'll exit [this book] changed."
—Frank Rutledge

Armchair Locomotion

poems by
Jen May

Empty-Grave Publishing

Copyright 2016 © Jen May

All rights reserved.

Cover design by Adam Nicolai
Published by Empty-Grave Publishing

ISBN: 1-62089-016-X
ISBN-13: 978-1-62089-016-5

Dedicated to family who have always been,
to longtime friends and new,
to hope, to kindness,
and to love.

CONTENTS

SENTINELS : 9
DAY TRAIN : 10
MORNING : 12
JOINING : 13
THE ONLY ONE : 14
SECRETS : 15
EL TOWN : 17
SUNDAY DRIVING ON THURSDAY : 18
WATER SIGN : 20
RECIPE : 21
FORBIDDEN WINE : 22
THIS MISSING : 23
WAITING ROOM : 24
TAKE ME TO : 25
LOVERS : 26
FOR YOU : 27
DO WE LOVE NOW? : 28

SUNDAY : 29

RENEWAL : 31

SPRING REVOLUTION : 32

STORM FRONT : 34

ATTENTION DEFICIT : 35

LIBRARY : 36

A DIFFERENT SORT OF GIVING TREE : 37

TIME CHANGE, A LATIN BAND : 38

AUTUMN PAIRING : 39

UPON THE DEATH OF JIM HARRISON : 40

CAVE DWELLER : 41

TURNING IN : 42

FALLING : 43

THERAPY : 44

OVER TIME : 45

KITCHEN WINDOW : 47

About the Author : 48

Sentinels

Mourning doves
perch wistfully in pairs
on melancholy murky mornings
just two or twelve
they post on the branches
gray and steady like sculptures—
patient and unmovable.

Day Train

Train brakes whistle, breaking
over the morning
and the rising sun breaks yolk-like
running messy and pooling
at our feet.
We hurry into the day,
hot coffee and phones in hand,
hardly noticing the slow rolling
but unconsciously we balance
against the reluctant train wake.
No surprise as we move now.
Gaining speed. No worry of
derailment or death
we ride bored,
some sleeping
into the day oblivious
of each other.
We run on like sentences,
like speeches
and video rolling.
Too hard.
To try.
Too sure.
To cry
out
and it rumbles
and rolls on

down the clack track
hung up on nothing
breeze by, shoot by
we wake now
and lumber on.
Lumber slow
and tired.
Until the doors
open and we
pour out
limply
into the day
as it breaks
over our heads.

Morning

Jammed into these accomplishing minutes
in the rush of hectic
my healing moments escape and I
have no time to help you or answer the phone
because I am already plugged in
with force—
and I can't find the place with my
second hand.

Joining

Screwed and soldered,
sealed and braced,
cemented, wildly taped or plugged—
I admire where things are joined.
How many layers of tile and ceiling?
Steel and glass
contain
contain me.

I don't want to fall up.
I belong where the brick lies,
where the train ties,
where we are bound.

The Only One

My secret fear
when walking from place to place
in the city (new buildings)
is the cranes that lift plates of glass
arcing high overhead
slip and drop one
into the street below.

I don't worry the landing
but the fear of the shattering
shakes me.

Bits of glass with momentum,
particles peppering bodies
like birdshot—

and the thing that really gets me
is nobody else
looks up.

Secrets

Push this piano
off the rooftop.
As it falls
I fall
into eternity
and the taxi slows—
someone left my shoe
in the road.

"Chair or no chair: a binary relation. But the vicissitudes of moving the body around are infinite. You never know what a person in a chair can do."

—Sarah Manguso

El Town

Enormous anonymity
this city and painful
evening chatter
casual or internal.
Stiff with the thunderous
motion, you too
are captive on the train.
With the woman and her wine
dropping popcorn
down her blouse,
or the scowling hipster,
or the teen couple in the corner
seat; do you all wipe your
smiles down your necks?
And you with your shoes shined,
with your hair clipped
and tipped—
I listen to your public talk
and I see how you smoke
in your car with your
hand out the window
so no one will know
but it all smells of
low rumble
and radio static
enough to tune
you out.

Sunday Driving on Thursday

I set off with the lap belt
buckle broken undone
in the copper-n-cream
'71 Olds convertible
a lot haywire
a little wanderlust
with jeans, Chucks and shirt untucked
I roll the miles highly
ease the curves
with the breeze streaming
and sunshine pouring like hot bronze
over my achy bones
I imagine the knotted muscle strings
of my back and shoulders come undone
like the wisps of hair tugging free
of my ballcap
and you are here
and you are here
and you are uninvited
mindful of no time passing
just road and cloud
cornstalk and hawk
oceans of soybean
and the oak trees lighthouse warnings
but I pay no attention

here I loose my tension
the forward motion
gently lapping
and rocking
this nutmeg yacht
the forward pulling
minutes into treasured moments
and the furrowed field of my brows
relax and sink
into a perfect neutral.

Water Sign

I am foremost rain.
Constant abiding
soaking love drenched quencher.
I am ocean
infinitely deep
secret and silent.
I am rush and hiss
rush and hiss
rush and hiss—
shove crash whitewater
cold and fast
clear, violent eroding.
I am hot spring
steaming passion
but I am tears loss
sliding, saturating all.

Recipe

Hope is an appetite, a craving for
coaxing flavors
prepping, peace and I'm centered
grounding, melting down
to a sizzle on the flame
and the flavors rise
the smells creep
peppers and onions, turn the pan
sear the juice in
and hold, hold there
before I burn.

Forbidden Wine

the glass of wine
forbidden
the grape tired hush
of secret sweetness
a simple drip of dew
on the leaf, then vine
purple red crush between
fingers cling to my
hand and underfoot slip
slow death and strained
I will reach for again

This Missing

The doorbell un-rung sounds vacant like
my coat slipping off the hanger slowly.

The hallway clock ticking sounds constant like
dripping bathwater on the floor.

Dust on my headboard sounds wistful like
pressing the pen on the page or
the breeze of my papers flipping uncaught.

Your voice imagined sounds raw like
the cursor blinking and I'm
pushing my fingers against my temples.

I'm scraping the chair
I'm smashing my plate on the tile.

I'm seeking in the empty space under the covers.

My skin untouched sounds dry like
rasping a straw for the last sip.

Waiting Room

Everything him is me
after a long time waiting in the hall
with the checkered floor
I cross and uncross my legs.
Bite my lips raw.
I would change my life,
fix new air,
learn new language,
to heal what broke at a word.
For a whisper
my life swings on a cobweb.

Take Me To

love, I reach for your hand
take me to the settled place
where you and I fold together
still as stars

take me to the quiet bees
and soundless prairie grass
bring me by the hushed marshland
walk its edge undefined and slowly
show me the quieted dawn
where mute
we speak only with love
faintly and inhibited

Lovers

Fold over me and under me
with your skin, linen paper
my sigh heard by only the walls and us,
I crush against you in a heavy afternoon perfume
your hands all ways on my body
stringing delight like paper lanterns
your frame – a climbing ladder for
    me to grasp higher and higher
your need for me, your skin all ways
    touching my skin
fold and crease, hold me now
hesitate no more, just lift and lift me against you
fold, doubling and loving
fold and press close now. Temple to temple
fold over me and under me
delicate like origami
until we envelop each other.

For You

Tree of grief, yes,
weeping willow,
wail and drape your hair low.
I want to wear your branches
back-straight
over my shoulders cape-like
and regally.

I would twine your twigs
to wreath my head
and crown myself,
in memoriam.

I want to lie at your root
and dream, while you
weep over me.
Bend and hang your curtain lower,
I haven't felt your tears yet.

Your trunk is stoic, straight,
unyielding.
I look up to you
with my leaves turned over
waiting for rain.

Do We Love Now?

Face to face your words hot as if a million suns
burn within my body
your lips press to my lips
give, give a touch
fingers comb your hair like summer's breeze
arch your back – cool now
kiss along my collarbone – bare now
cup and lift my breasts
nipples scrape, hard against your palms

hold, hold to revel – hold
hold to love

and just as your gentle gives way
to urgency
my tease turns to take
we die a little and breathe

with the assurance of seasons
we will love together
more and more again
greedy drunk
and listening to our shared
heart rhythms

Sunday

easy chair coffee window drip
lazy crossword puzzle muffin in
the oven
deck puddle nuzzle nap duvet
stretch head to foot no yoga
lamp turned low
paint peeling on the ceiling
rolling sound out loud by the
tongue
feet tangled all angles

"Truth is not fully explosive, but purely electric. You don't blow the world up with the truth; you shock it into motion."

—Criss Jami, *Healology*

Renewal

Bald spring,
ugly spring.
Stirring March winds
rouse the trash left after snow melt and
plants it along fences –
hedges of waste.

Dirty spring
gray road salt scrubs roadways down,
rough sponge bath style
but grime spatters all over with the old bird bath water.

Rough spring
like a sucker punch split lip
bleed icy spit in the face
or the mist covers everything like secrets
and wears a frost bandage the next morning.

Restless
spring into action
running running
drip drop repeat
bone damp chill

but robin call
whitetail walk cautious
startle spring
and bulb shoot needles
green up
warm comfort spring
coming.

Spring Revolution

Thaw today—
we shed wool coats
carry them prickling
over our rolled sleeves.

Still in winter blacks
we are mismatched
in the clinging sunshine.

The first sweat this work
work how we may
we raise our pinched faces
to the spring life lift.

We're tossing our hair back with abandon
animated in the melt season—
the mud season.

A man crouches
tying up his laces,
turns up his dragging cuffs,
keeping them from puddled hopes
on the asphalt.

Twigs scrape windows
as if wanting an invitation
for the huffing stirring wind
the whining wind
the grasping knocking wind
that sifts and sends the throw-away
trash careening.

Bags and newspapers blow
to far off fences,
where they line up
and wait for the clean-up crew.

Storm Front

Each time this change comes
it comes noticeably
it stirs
it stirs us
when the jet stream bends
our way and the sky
weaves a storm front darkening
so the distant lightning strikes
against cadet blue fields
air cools – plunging cold

like blanching beans
bright green and crisp.

Attention Deficit

I can't seem to concentrate on the words
when flipping pages of dusty favorites
in the home grown bookstore cafe
with guitar strums and chords and
the echo of the slap of her flats on the yellowing tile
among the piles of
The Cigar Aficionado's Buying Guide,
Ferrets for Dummies,
Chocolate Maker Dreams,
and the AC kicks into high gear
though it's cool outside and fluttery
like Marilyn Monroe's poster eyelashes.
Mr. Anyman over there checks his cash
and his wife checks her nails
and their kids knock shelves with their
wrestling moves
and the owner is tapping impatiently
like get the hell out of my place—
what are you doing here anyway?
while the life-size Carmen Miranda
with her hooped earrings as big as bracelets
sells palm trees to the customers
with a sugar cane smile
and a drop of milk for your coffee.

Library

Just dusk in the Midwest
my book lying open in the last
light and the type lines remind me
of cornrows.
I harvest them as I read aloud
the way my tongue and teeth
collaborate to form each word,
coddle it to life and lift it.
Or gush it from my mouth
like great combines
forming corn kernel pyramids
to point heaven high.
After dark
the text doesn't matter so much
as the twist-roll, loll
and spittle tap
brightly lit in farm song night.

A Different Sort of Giving Tree

I approach it as a fight, I size it up.
Seizing a branch just within reach, I
pull myself to it and
scrape my sneakers, peeling the loose bark.
I scramble for a foothold.
Unsuccessful, I slip down and the
earth pillows my rough landing.

Lifting my chin defiantly, I
reach higher, hold tighter. Lift and struggle.
Scrape along that thick trunk. I try.
My shoe sticks, pulling harder, I wriggle over
the lowest branch.

Looking for my next handhold,
I stretch to the next footing. Splay my arms and
push with my short legs. Kneescrape, one branch higher.

Apples hail on me and honeybees rocket but I don't let go.
I compete for one more higher. Push again.
The whole tree shakes while I find my comfortable limbseat.

Now victorious, my hands red and dirty, I grasp on to steady me
– the rough queen of my apple tree.
I reign small from this throne in my backyard home.

Breeze flutters my subject leaves, rustling like silks in the spotted shade.
I am mussed and streaky but the greens bow anyway.

Then my shoulder gives over, drowsy tired.
Finally cool here I lean, for a long while.

I can rest here? Close my eyes: I am sheltered within
having occupied this at least this territory.

Time Change, A Latin Band

Every year I look to the spring forward and falling back
it's a long guitar melody, sexy

but playing on and on
while the drummer maintains the rhythm
and the front man introduces the pieces

red maracas for shh shh shh and conga beat blossoms for flavor
rich purple bass, feel it in your feet, soles on the floor
so that sweet wail guitar
the cry of stretched time passing
with the tambourine clatter clash
some small sweat
or some chill voice sing

the air expanding breath
and deflating exhale

Do we win? Or are we tied, snarled,
defeated by the hour
the minute, the moment
we change?

Autumn Pairing

Paired with the new coolness
crispy and tangy
apple cider fresh
the murmuration of starlings
that twist and swoop in waves
and paintbrush treetops
drip color on the asphalt canvas.
You grasp to hold on in the saxophone gale.
It is the making of together or alone,
the most vibrant death—
torn bread, hot and crusty
pushed together again to heal
the crops taken in and field turned.
Autumn is the echo of a woodpecker
tap on the cedar siding
but mist rises silent from the muddy plain
lonely teacup steaming
with warm spices
sips somber like a flat piano
played with flannel fingers.

"There is a human wildness held beneath the skin
that finds all barriers brutishly unbearable."

                  -Jim Harrison, from "Arts"
                      Songs of Unreason

Upon the Death of Jim Harrison

Released. You are released to light whispers
and moonlight rivers.
Your poems high-scavenging words from eagle aeries
and young feather-down lines the canyon crags of your face.
Primitive man you explored the river flood and flux
against the mountainside stone faces with deft
landscape scribbles
and the intention of horses, insects and dogs.
Read to me the melody of your poems – I'm listening
to the cows and darkness, your non-lament
about youth and death
an observer of cycles or pain, big as the
universe shock of a cigarette scar
tiny to your brain and soft like trout and pine needles
about beautiful ugly mothers and eggs
but always returning to the river.

Always returning to the river,
you are released.

Cave Dweller

In the cool dampness
of the mine tunnel,
when I was nine—

I held my father's hand
and crowded behind his leg.

The tour walked on and I stayed behind
dazzled by the sparkling points.
I timidly reached out
to pin my finger with the tip
and caressed the crystals
hoping to imbue myself
with magic or God.

This is the place
where I gathered rich fragments.

The cave of memory,
the silence of alone and
the curiosity of youth.

I held the gems up
to the light of introspection.
Curious.

Turning In

Momma leans over me
pulling another blanket up
and tucks the sides.

I know she means to shield me.
She reads over me.
I nestle in.
I catch her as she blesses me
and kisses my forehead saying

dream well for this night will give you
tomorrow's horizon.

Falling

When I have the dream about falling.
When I have the dream about falling it's on these stairs.

These stairs
where you and I were once.
Where we said goodbye
and broke our hearts on the landing.

These stairs.
Where we were once.

Where I came and went every day for years
and then I was gone.
Then you were gone.

The falling.
With the feeling of uneasy love
and you and I were there once.
When I have the dream about falling
where you and I
where you and I fell.

In the dream.
In the dream.

Falling
always falling again.

Therapy

This time I will close my eyes
while you pass your hands before me.

A ritual of cleansing.

The ritual of slow memory.

Armchair locomotion.

Over Time

Time runs slow into a slow ruin
An apple fallen, half rot
the squeeze underfoot
spoken softly in the no-corner of the mind
smells like a hint of silver mirrored decay.

Who can see this wreckage?
Who knows this certain ache?

I pulse with vigor and then retract
beaten down by moments of loss.

of heartbreak

My joys subside
unmeasured and seeping past foundations
through thick cement walls
rooting, no, — anchoring there with the strength of tall trees
freeze and thaw
cracks open and crumble

My homes ground to dust
and ashy grit
there is risk in remaining unmoved here

so I try to gather myself again.

"But you might as well bid a man struggling in the water, rest within arm's length of the shore! I must reach it first, and then I'll rest."

—Emily Brontë, *Wuthering Heights*

Kitchen Window

You can't know what it's like to be a woman
balancing on the edge of herself
running on the shoulder of chaos daily.
So you will walk the thin line of your mind until
you trip up on the carpet and the chandelier
clinks soft warnings before smashing to the floor.
Sometimes as you wash the dishes
you daydream of breaking the kitchen window
but you know that sudden displays of violence
will cause the whole circus to fall in.
How much can you take before you say
enough and make them acknowledge
what they have done to you?

Jen May is a poet warrior. As a former police officer, she has witnessed much grief and inhumanity. As a writer and warrior, she refuses to give up hope.

Jen May is a founding member of Open Sky Poets in the Fox Valley, Illinois region. You may have seen her read at an open mic at A-Town Poetics or Harmonious Howl. She has been a featured reader at Waterline Writers, Lit by the Bridge, and Mutual Ground's Survivor's Art Show. Jen has previously served as editor of two fine arts magazines, *Byzantium* and *Towers*. Most recently, she has been published in the *Journal of Modern Poetry 19: Poetry of Protest*.

Visit her blog www.JenMayPoems.com for posts on the arts, charity, compassionate humanism, words, writing prompts, and poetic form. Look for her next book *Battle Cry*, coming soon.

An excerpt from the forthcoming:
Battle Cry

Anatomy Lesson

I wear apologies in my eyes daily.
And I draw red loneliness on my lips,
    to tell you the truth about my mouth.
I have scolded my hands for writing again.
And the grief of my spine slumps, exhausted.
I can't raise my head because I'm closing
off words in my throat.
I shift in my seat and hold my sweater—
    small comfort, like a blanket.
But don't mistake me for weak or easy.
Or I'll strike you with my knee—
for I won't stand to call myself
broken much longer.

www.ingramcontent.com/pod-product-compliance
Lightning Source LLC
Chambersburg PA
CBHW061346040426
42444CB00011B/3110